GEOGRAPHY OF THE WORLD

THE LAND OF THE

ANDES

By Barbara A. Somervill

THE CHILD'S WORLD®
CHANHASSEN, MINNESOTA

The Child's World

Published in the United States of America by The Child's World®
PO Box 326, Chanhassen, MN 55317-0326
800-599-READ
www.childsworld.com

Content Adviser:
Mark Williams,
Associate Professor,
University of Colorado,
Boulder, Colorado

Photo Credits: Cover/frontispiece: Galen Rowell/Corbis.
Interior: Animals Animals/Earth Scenes: 11 (Paul A. Jenkins), 18 (Erwin & Peggy Bauer); Corbis: 9 (Theo Allofs), 12 (Larry Lee Photography), 13 (Staffan Widstrand), 15 (Wolfgang Kaehler), 17 (Douglas Peebles), 19 (Anders Ryman), 23 (Julie Houck); Stuart Franklin/Magnum Photos: 5, 6, 25, 26; Thomas Hoepker/Magnum Photos: 14; Travelsite/Colasanti/Picture Desk: 4, 8; Travelsite/Dagli Orti/Picture Desk: 21.

The Child's World®: Mary Berendes, Publishing Director

Editorial Directions, Inc.: E. Russell Primm, Editorial Director; Melissa McDaniel, Line Editor; Katie Marsico, Associate Editor; Judi Shiffer, Associate Editor and Library Media Specialist; Matthew Messbarger, Editorial Assistant; Susan Hindman, Copy Editor; Sarah E. De Capua and Lucia Raatma, Proofreaders; Marsha Bonnoit, Peter Garnham, Terry Johnson, Olivia Nellums, Chris Simms, Katherine Trickle, and Stephen Carl Wender, Fact Checkers; Tim Griffin/IndexServ, Indexer; Cian Loughlin O'Day, Photo Researcher; Linda S. Koutris, Photo Selector; XNR Productions, Inc., Cartographer

The Design Lab: Kathleen Petelinsek, Design and Page Production

Library of Congress Cataloging-in-Publication Data
Somervill, Barbara A.
  The land of the Andes / by Barbara A. Somervill.
    p. cm. — (Geography of the world series)
  Includes index.
  ISBN 1-59296-331-5 (library bound : alk. paper) 1. Andes—Juvenile literature.
I. Title. II. Series.
  F2212.S66 2004
  918—dc22   2004003724

TABLE OF CONTENTS

CHAPTER ONE

TO HONOR THE SUN GOD

High in the Andes Mountains sits the city of Cuzco, Peru. During the last week of June, thousands of people flock to Cuzco. They make the journey to enjoy a special event: Inti Raymi.

Cuzco, Peru, sprawls across a high plain in the Andes.

Before Europeans arrived in South America, the Incan people controlled Peru. For centuries, the Incas honored their sun god, Inti, on the winter solstice, the shortest day of the year. During Inti Raymi, they feasted on corn, potatoes, and coca tea. They prayed that Inti would

The Inti Raymi festival honors the Inca sun god, called Inti.

bring spring and bless their fields with good crops. Inti Raymi was the highlight of the long Andean winter. But after the Spanish conquered the Incas, Inti Raymi was banned.

Today, the people of Cuzco again celebrate Inti Raymi. Live music has locals and visitors dancing in the streets. Plays recall the greatness of the Incan culture. Parades wind their way to an ancient Incan fortress. As the sun sets, a new year begins in the Andes.

CHAPTER TWO

THE MAKING OF A MOUNTAIN RANGE

Earth has built mountains since time began. It is part of the ever-changing nature of our planet. But it is a very slow process.

The earth makes mountains in different ways. Volcanoes, earthquakes, incredible pressure, and collisions can produce mountains. Like most mountain ranges, the Andes resulted from a mix of these processes.

High grasslands in the Andes are called altiplano.

The continents and the seafloor make up the outer shell of earth, called the crust. Earth's crust is not an unbroken layer like an orange peel. Instead, it has cracks. These cracks divide the crust into about 20 different pieces, called plates. These plates are constantly moving. In places where two plates are pushing against each other, mountains are built. In other places, one plate slides under another. This process is called subduction. It also builds mountains.

To better understand subduction, try this experiment: Place two paper plates on a counter. Put one face up and the other face down. Slide the face-down paper plate under the face-up plate. What happens? The face-up plate rises, just like the Andes did.

Two hundred million years ago, dinosaurs roamed the land. Birds and flowers first appeared on earth. Around this same time, the Nazca Plate in the Pacific Ocean began to slide under the South American Plate. The Nazca Plate shifted only a few inches a year. It took about 75 million years, but this slow movement built the Andes. The plate collision is still occurring today.

Volcanoes also build mountains. Eruptions spew hot lava that cools to form solid rock. As the rock piles up, it builds land. Eventually, enough volcanic rock builds up to form a mountain. Dozens of volcanoes in the Andes are currently building mountains.

Active volcanoes such as Chile's Parinacota erupt rarely. Farmers grow vegetables on the fields near this volcano.

Scientists can tell how a mountain was made by studying the rock that it is made of. Plate collisions cause the formation of spectacular volcanic eruptions. The lava that erupts forms incredibly thick layers of volcanic rock in Chile and Peru. The active volcanoes in the

When a sheet of ice breaks off a glacier's end, the process is called calving.

Andes provide scientists with the evidence that the Nazca Plate is still colliding with the South American Plate.

Glaciers can change the look of a mountain. Between 10,000 and 12,000 years ago, massive ice sheets stretched across much of South America. This happened toward the end of the Great Ice Age, which began about 1.6 million years ago. The weight and pressure of the glaciers ground solid rock into dust. The glaciers also carved valleys, dug riverbeds, and bulldozed flat plains across the land.

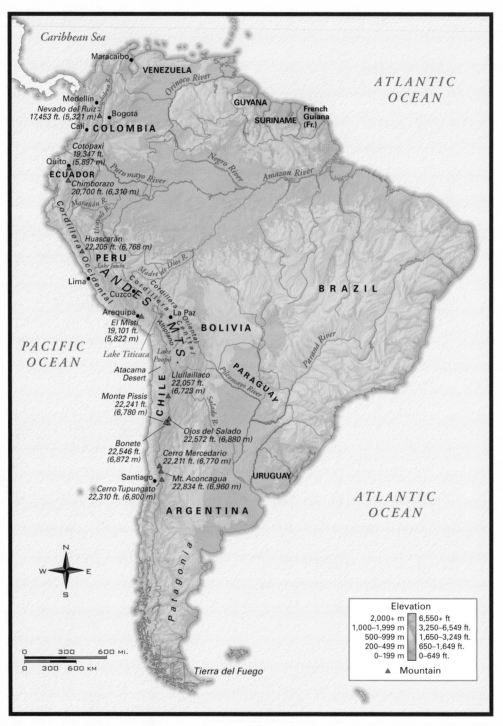

A map of the Andes

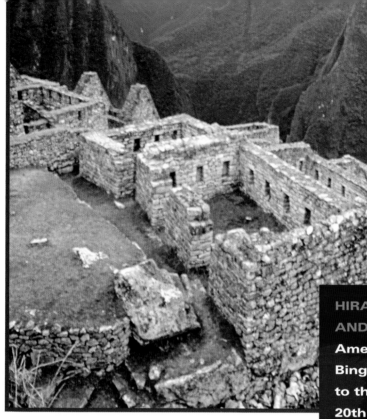

Machu Picchu remained a mystery until the explorations of Hiram Bingham in 1911.

The Andes run north to south for about 4,500 miles (7,200 kilometers), from the southern tip of South America all the way to the Caribbean Sea. In between are grasslands, **rain forests,** deserts, and glaciers. Every **habitat** you can think of, from dense jungle to empty wasteland, exists in the Andes.

CHAPTER THREE

ABOUT THE ANDES

The Andes Mountains stretch the length of South America—and then some. The Andes begin under water in the southern Atlantic Ocean. The mountains rise above the water in Tierra del Fuego, at the southern tip of South America, and run the length of the continent. They end in Venezuela at the Caribbean Sea.

The Andes is not one mountain range, but several grouped together. The three main ranges are the **Cordillera** Occidental, the Cordillera Central, and the Cordillera Oriental. Smaller ranges cut through the main cordilleras. Dozens of peaks in the Andes rise more than 20,000 feet (6,100 meters). The highest peak in the Andes is

The rugged peaks of Tierra del Fuego rise in the southern Andes.

Aconcagua, which rises 22,834 feet (6,960 m) in western Argentina. Other towering Andean mountains are Ojos del Salado (22,572 feet/6,880 m) and Bonete (22,546 feet/6,872 m).

In the Andes, climate and **ecosystems** change from east to west. The Andes' eastern foothills host

Colorful hoatzin feast on flowers, leaves, and fruits in Peru's Manú National Park.

Water in the Atacama Desert comes mainly from underground springs such as this hot springs geyser near Tatio.

dense rain forests. To the west lies the Atacama, the world's driest desert. In the Atacama, 20 years can pass without a single raindrop touching the ground. Between these two extremes lie rich valleys, sheer peaks, and rushing rivers.

As the snow in the Andes melts, it feeds hundreds of rivers. The fabled Amazon River and the majestic Orinoco River begin in the Andes. Major rivers heading east include the Ucayali, Marañón, Tigre, Napa, Putumayo, and Madre de Dios. Argentina's Paraná, Salado, and Negro rivers also flow eastward from the Andes. Rivers flowing to the Pacific Ocean are fewer and smaller.

The world's highest major lake—Lake Titicaca—lies between Bolivia and Peru. Big ships and tiny one-person boats made of reeds sail Lake Titicaca, which lies 12,507 feet (3,812 m) above sea level. Other large Andean lakes include Bolivia's Poopó and Peru's Junín.

CHAPTER FOUR

PLANTS AND ANIMALS
OF THE ANDES

The Andes environment supports a huge variety of plants and animals. A few **species** manage to survive in the bone-dry Atacama Desert. Rain forests, on the other hand, explode with life. There are brilliant orchids and wildflowers, snakes and lizards, bats and bugs, bugs, bugs.

Delicate white orchids wave in the breezes of Aguas Calientes Park.

The desert regions of the Andes—the Atacama and bleak Patagonia—support little life. Cacti and scruffy grasses dot the landscape. In the summer, calandrina, malvilla, and ananuca bloom, even though no rain falls. Lizards, worms, and a few mammals venture onto the Andean deserts. All living things depend on water. In the Andean deserts, water comes as gentle mists blowing off the Pacific Ocean.

Another dry region in the Andes is the *altiplano,* a vast high grassland. Camel-like creatures—llamas, alpacas, vicuñas, and guanacos—graze on ichu grasses. Andean condors circle overhead, searching for dead animals on which to feed. The altiplano supports lizards, rodents, deer, and flightless birds called tinamous.

THE ANDEAN CONDOR

Andean condors are the largest birds in South America. Their wings are nearly 10 feet (3 m) across. Condors feed on dead animals. With their excellent eyesight, the birds soar overhead searching for their favorite foods: guanacos, alpacas, and penguins.

Unlike the dry deserts and plains, the Andean rain forests are wet, wet, wet. Some regions receive more than 200 inches (5 m) of rain a year. So many critters and plants live in the rain forests that scientists have not discovered them all. There are tens of thousands of insect species alone. But lots of other creatures also enjoy the rain forest's plenty. Howler monkeys, tamarins, and marmosets make their homes in monkey puzzle trees. Hummingbirds dart from blossom to blossom among the thousands of orchids, bromeliads, and figs.

Patagonia is a remote desert region in the southern Andes.

Sleek jaguars stalk agoutis and tapirs. In the rain forest, blood-sucking leeches can grow to 2 feet (61 centimeters) long. Blood-sucking vampire bats also thrive, along with other bats that eat fruit and insects.

The Andes have an odd mix of unused land and overused land. Few people live on high mountain peaks, in the Atacama, or in Patagonia. These areas are surprisingly delicate and need to be protected from air and water pollution and wasteful mining.

The Andean plains and valleys, on the other hand, have been home to humans for several thousand years. Long ago, forests were cleared to make room to graze herds and raise crops. This land cannot be returned to the wild because it feeds and supports people. Water and air pollution and industrial waste create problems in these regions, too.

THE JAGUAR

The jaguar is the largest **predator** in the Andes. It lives alone, deep in the rain forest. Unlike many cats, the jaguar is an excellent swimmer and will follow its prey into the water. Jaguars eat agoutis, tapirs, capybaras, fish, frogs, turtles, and caimans. They will also kill cattle, llamas, and goats. Some ranchers will do anything to protect their herds. They have killed so many jaguars that only a few of these powerful cats remain.

Jaguars are the largest predators in the Andes.

Rain forests and cloud forests have been misused and abused. Millions of acres of forest have been destroyed as people cut trees for timber and dig gold mines. As the forests disappear, wild creatures lose their homes.

Engineers have carved terraces in this Bolivian mountainside to mine gold.

Protecting the environment has become a major issue in the Andes. Every Andean country has established national parks and wildlife preserves. But many of these parks do not actually protect the land and wildlife. They are listed as preserves, but officials allow logging, mining, and hunting to continue. These activities provide jobs and money for people in the Andes. But these activities also damage the environment. In the Andes, finding a balance between what is good for people and what is good for nature has been difficult.

CHAPTER FIVE

THE PEOPLE OF THE ANDES

People have lived in the Andes for about 12,000 years. These early people lived in family groups called clans. Over time, these clans grew and combined. Different cultures emerged, such as the Nazca, the Quitus, and the Tiahuanaco. They built cities and farmed the land.

In about A.D. 1200, a new civilization began. These were the Incas. The word *Inca* means "leader." For many years, the Incas remained in the mountain valley that surrounded their capital city, Cuzco. But by the 1400s, the Incas began flexing their muscles. They conquered many other native cultures. Within a century, the Incas ruled nearly 32 million people. Cuzco was the center of Incan life.

In the Incan world, everyone was expected to work, and few went hungry. Everyone paid taxes to the chief Inca, called the Sapa Inca. Those taxes fed the hungry, built roads, and improved agriculture.

The Incan culture survived until the Spanish arrived in the early 1500s. The Spanish brought with them serious European diseases, such as measles and smallpox, which were new to the people of South America. Disease raced through the Andes, killing many native people. In 1532, the Spanish conquered the Incas and began changing the world of the Andes.

This 17th-century church brought the architecture of Spain to Peru.

One thing that changed was religion. Most Spanish were Roman Catholic. They hoped to convert the Indians to their religion. Today, more than 90 percent of the people in the Andes are Roman Catholic.

The Andes today are home to about one-third of the people in South America. Most are descendants of both the Incas and the Spanish.

How people live in the Andes depends on whether they live in the city or the country. In cities such as Lima, Peru; Quito, Ecuador; and Bogotá, Colombia, people live much as they do in North American cities. They live in houses or apartments and work in banks, factories, and schools. They are doctors and lawyers, police officers and firefighters, teachers and cooks. They wake up to radio stations playing their favorite songs. At night, they watch soccer on television or read the newspaper. Most city dwellers in the Andes speak Spanish or Portuguese.

QUITO

Quito, Ecuador, is the oldest capital city in South America. Quito lies near the equator. Most places near the equator are warm year-round. But the climate of Quito is more like that of rainy, chilly England. Quito has a cool climate because it is 9,350 feet (2,850 m) above sea level. The name *Quito* comes from the Quitus people who lived in the region during the 11th century.

People who live in rural areas are called campesinos, which means country folk. They are much more likely to be descended from native peoples. Most speak native languages such as Quechua or Aymara. For them, Spanish is a foreign language.

Mountain living hasn't changed much in 500 years. Campesinos live in small huts, often with only one or two rooms. Many campesinos have no running water, plumbing, or electricity. The people rise with the sun and work all day. They grow crops or tend herds of cows, sheep, or llamas. They survive on what they grow and make for

Peruvian natives buy their vegetables at weekly open markets.

themselves. The children work the family farm. When planting or harvesting needs to be done, children may not go to school. Mountain communities are close-knit. If families need help, their neighbors provide.

Some parts of the modern world have reached the campesinos. They can buy clothing and shoes. And most families listen to their favorite soccer team's games on battery-powered radios.

There is not a lot of industry in the Andes. One of the biggest industries is mining. Bolivia mines silver, tin, zinc, lead, copper, and tungsten. The mines provide most of the country's **exports** but employ only three in one hundred workers. Chile mines copper, sulfur, coal, and iron ore. Here, too, mining accounts for half the country's exports but provides jobs for only two workers in one hundred. Peru has rich deposits of copper, silver, lead, zinc, and iron. Oil has made some people in Colombia and Venezuela rich.

Agriculture is important in the Andes. Argentina is a world leader in producing wheat, rye, and corn. Peru grows potatoes, wheat, corn, and barley. Colombia is known for outstanding coffee, cotton, rice, and bananas. Unfortunately, the wealth from mining and agriculture is not spread around. The average worker is paid very little.

The largest cash crop in the Andes is illegal: cocaine. Illegal coca, the base for cocaine, is a serious problem in Colombia, Ecuador, Peru, and Bolivia. The war on drugs has had little impact. Unfortunately, for people in the Andes, growing coca is a way to put food on the table. Andean farmers can earn more from one coca crop than from a lifetime of farming potatoes or corn.

CHAPTER SIX

THE CULTURE OF THE ANDES

What a difference 100 miles (160 km) makes for the people of the Andes. People who live in cities have telephones and computers. They watch television, go dancing, and eat out at fast-food restaurants. City dwellers have schools, hospitals, libraries, movie theaters, malls, and supermarkets.

Rural living is different. There are no restaurants for quick take-out meals. Television is rare. Dancing is part of a harvest celebration, a

Modern Lima was founded in 1535 by Spanish conquistador Francisco Pizarro.

FROZEN MUMMIES

In 1999, Dr. Johan Reinhard led a team that found three frozen mummies on an Andean peak 22,000 feet (6,800 m) high. The mummies were Incan children whose bodies had been wrapped and put on a burial platform 500 years earlier. The bodies were surrounded by gifts to the Incan gods, including gold and silver statues, pottery, and food. Because of the freezing temperatures, the bodies were perfectly preserved—they still had hair on their arms. Scientists can learn much about Incan life by studying the mummies' clothing, muscles, hair, and bones.

wedding, or a birthday. Most entertainment comes from family and village celebrations.

Open market days provide a chance to sell extra crops and crafts. It is also a good time to catch up on gossip. The scents of grilled meat and corn-on-the-cob fill the air. Expert weavers display colorful cloth. A

A farmer's market in the Andes offers vegetables, crafts, and livestock.

potter makes a large jug on a pottery wheel. Shoppers pore over medicinal herbs, leather goods, dried fish, and piles of potatoes. The weekly market is the campesino supermarket.

Some aspects of life in the Andes are the same whether you live in the city or the country. No matter where you live, family and the church are central. Major life events—births, marriages, and deaths—are shared among family and friends.

Many South American social events are connected with the Roman Catholic Church. Saint's day celebrations, Christmas, and Easter are not just religious holidays. They are national holidays during which banks, post offices, and businesses close. Parades wind down broad city boulevards and narrow village streets. Panpipes, drums, and flutes fill the air. Everywhere the rhythm of life beats in the songs of the Andes.

CELEBRATING A HAIRCUT
One celebration unique to the Andes is that of the first haircut, called the *rutuchicoy.* In Incan days, a first haircut was an important celebration. The family received gifts during the rutuchicoy. That still happens today, only the gifts are usually money. The cash is placed in the bank for the child's future needs.

Glossary

cloud forest (KLOUD FOR-ist)
A cloud forest is a wet mountain forest that is usually covered in fog and mist. Peru's Manú Biosphere Reserve is one of several protected cloud forests in the Andes.

cordillera (kor-dih-YER-uh) A cordillera is a long mountain range. The Andes are made up of three main cordilleras.

ecosystems (EE-koh-siss-tuhmz) An ecosystem is the community of plants, animals, water, and soil located in one area, which work together as a unit. The Andes support a variety of ecosystems.

equator (ei-KWAY-tur) The equator is an imaginary line around earth exactly halfway between the North and the South Pole. The equator runs through Ecuador, Brazil, and Colombia.

exports (EK-sports) Exports are things that are sent from one country to another country. About half of Chile's exports come from mining.

glaciers (GLAY-shurz) Glaciers are huge sheets of moving ice. Thousands of years ago, the movement of glaciers carved out valleys and riverbeds in the Andes.

habitat (HAB-uh-tat) A habitat is a place where a plant or animal normally lives. The Andes supports a huge variety of habitats.

predator (PRED-uh-tur) A predator is an animal that hunts and eats other animals. The jaguar is the largest predator in the Andes.

rain forests (RAYN FOR-ists)
Rain forests are regions that receive a lot of rain and usually have a very wide variety of plant and animal life. On the eastern side of the Andes lie dense rain forests.

species (SPEE-sheez) A species is a kind of plant or animal. Tens of thousands of species of insects live in the rain forests of the Andes.

An Andes Almanac

Extent

Length: About 4,500 miles (7,200 km)

Width: 400 miles (640 km)

Continent: South America

Countries: Argentina, Bolivia, Chile, Colombia, Ecuador, Peru, and Venezuela

Major ranges: Cordillera Central, Cordillera Occidental, and Cordillera Oriental

Major rivers: Amazon, Madre de Dios, Magdalena, Marañón, Napa, Negro, Orinoco, Paraná, Pilcomayo, Putumayo, Salado, Tigre, Ucayali, and Urubamba

Major lakes: Poopó, Titicaca (Bolivia); Junín (Peru)

Major cities: La Paz (Bolivia); Santiago (Chile); Bogotá, Cali, Medellin (Colombia); Quito (Ecuador), Arequipa, Cuzco, Lima (Peru); Maracaibo (Venezuela)

Major languages: Quechua and Spanish

High peaks:

Aconcagua	22,834 feet	(6,960 m)
Ojos del Salado	22,572 feet	(6,880 m)
Bonete	22,546 feet	(6,872 m)
Tupungato	22,310 feet	(6,800 m)
Pissis	22,241 feet	(6,780 m)
Mercedario	22,211 feet	(6,770 m)
Huascaran	22,205 feet	(6,768 m)

A total of 49 peaks higher than 20,000 feet (6,096 m)

Parks and preserves: Los Alerces, Los Glacieres, Nahuel Huapî (Argentina); Juan Fernandez, Lauca, Torres del Paine (Chile); Manú (Peru)

Natural resources: Copper, gold, iron ore, lead, petroleum, silver, timber, tin, tungsten, and zinc

Native birds: Andean condosr, Andean flamingos, black skimmers, caracaras, cock-of-the-rock, great horned owls, guans, huet-huet birds, macaws, parrots, and tinamous

Native mammals: Agoutis, alpacas, bats, capybaras, deer, guanacos, howler monkeys, jaguars, llamas, marmosets, spectacled bears, tamarins, tapirs, and vicuñas

Native reptiles: Caimans, lizards, and snakes
Native plants: Ananucas, bamboo, bromeliads, calandrinas, candelabra cacti, ferns, figs, ichu grasses, malvilla, monkey puzzle trees, mosses, and orchids

The Andes in the News

600 million years ago	The first mountain building period in Alpine region takes place.
200 million years ago	The Nazca Plate begins to slide under the South American Plate.
125 million years ago	The Andes become a full-fledged mountain range.
10,000–3000 B.C.	Early people live in the Andean valleys and foothills.
10,000 B.C.	Ice sheets cover parts of the Andes up to Ecuador.
A.D. 1200	The Incan civilization is founded. Cuzco is built.
1400s	The Incas conquer most of the Andes.
1532	The Spanish conquer the Incas.
1572	The Spanish ban Inti Raymi celebrations.
1811–1824	Wars for independence rage across South America. New nations established include Venezuela, Colombia, Ecuador, Peru, Bolivia, Chile, and Argentina.
1897	Swiss mountaineer Matthias Zurbriggen becomes the first European to climb Aconcagua.
1911	Explorer Hiram Bingham finds Machu Picchu in Peru's Andes.
1960s	Increased sale of illegal cocaine becomes a major economic and political issue throughout the Andes.
1973	Peru establishes the Manú Biosphere Reserve.
1985	Nevado del Ruiz erupts, killing more than 23,000 people.
1995	A border war erupts between Ecuador and Peru.
1999	A massive earthquake shakes Colombia, leaving 1,185 dead and 250,000 homeless. Dr. Johan Reinhard leads a team that finds three frozen mummies on an Andean peak 22,000 feet (6,700 m) high.
2001	A huge Incan burial ground is discovered outside Lima, Peru.

How to Learn More about the Andes

At The Library

NONFICTION

Blue, Rose, and Corrine Naden. *Andes Mountains.* Austin, Tex.: Raintree Steck-Vaughn, 1995.

Cobb, Vicki. *This Place Is High: The Andes Mountains of South America.* New York: Walker & Co., 1993.

Dwyer, Christopher. *Chile.* Broomall, Pa.: Chelsea House, 1997.

Everts, Tammy. *Peru: The People and Culture.* Toronto: Crabtree Press, 2003.

Getz, David. *Frozen Girl.* New York: Henry Holt & Company, Inc., 1998.

FICTION

Charles, Veronika Martenova. *Necklace of Stars.* Markham, Ontario: Fitzhenry & Whiteside, Ltd., 1997.

Palacios, Argentina. *The Llama's Secret.* Mahwah, N.J.: Troll, 1993.

On the Web

VISIT OUR HOME PAGE FOR LOTS OF LINKS ABOUT THE ANDES:

http://www.childsworld.com/links.html

Note to Parents, Teachers, and Librarians: We routinely verify our Web links to make sure they're safe, active sites—so encourage your readers to check them out!

Places to Visit or Contact

CHILEAN NATIONAL TOURIST BOARD

510 West 6th Street

Los Angeles, CA 90014

213/627-4293

COLOMBIAN CONSULATE

1825 Connecticut Avenue NW

Washington, DC 20009

202/332-7476

ECUADOR TOURIST BOARD

Call them toll-free at 800/ECUADOR (800/328-2367)

tourism@ecuadortouristboard.com

Index

About the Author

Barbara A. Somervill is the author of many books for children. She loves learning and sees every writing project as a chance to learn new information or gain a new understanding. Somervill grew up in New York State, but she has also lived in Toronto, Canada; Canberra, Australia; California; and South Carolina. She currently lives with her husband in Simpsonville, South Carolina.